before the bell rings

Alemany Press

OTHER TITLES OF INTEREST

ACTION ENGLISH PICTURES
Maxine Frauman-Prickel and Noriko Takahashi

THE ACTION REPORTER
Armando Riverol

BACK & FORTH
Adrian S. Palmer, Theodore S. Rodgers, with Judy W-B Olsen

BRIDGE THE GAP
Jami Ferrer and Patty Werner

THE CHILDREN'S RESPONSE
Caroline Linse

COMMUNICATION-STARTERS
Judy W-B Olsen

DRAWING OUT
Sharron Bassano and Mary Ann Christison

ENGLISH THROUGH DRAMA
John Dennis & Associates, Inc.

ENGLISH THROUGH POETRY
Mary Ann Christison

LOOK AGAIN PICTURES
Judy W-B Olsen

LOOK WHO'S TALKING!
Sharron Bassano and Mary Ann Christison

before the bell rings

gregory stricherz

Alemany Press
a division of
Janus Book Publishers, Inc.
Hayward, California

Printed in the United States of America.

ISBN 0-88084-131-1

7 8 9 0 1 2 3 4 D - P 0 9 8 7 6 5 4

Alemany Press

2501 Industrial Parkway West
Hayward, California 94545

TABLE OF CONTENTS

INTRODUCTION

Has your lesson plan ever ended five minutes before the bell rings? This book of listening practices is something you can pick up and use in just such a situation. No real preparation is necessary. Of course it can also be used at other times, too—perhaps as a brief change of pace during a lesson.

These Listening Practices emphasize understanding and following oral commands. There's also lots of practice with spatial relationships. Understanding oral commands and grasping spatial relationships are two skills most LEP students have difficulty with. By the time they finish this book they should be quite good in both areas.

As you work through this book you'll notice that some English skills such as spelling and sound discrimination are being practiced. My students sometimes tire of a steady diet of English skills but they've always seemed interested in number and line-drawing problems. So a lot of number and line-drawing problems are included. The math has been kept fairly simple though so that students aren't hindered by low math skills. Most probably will gain some facility in math from these practices however. You might want to point out to the students that the situations used in this book are not always commonly used. But the skills they gain from the practice are.

The practices are grouped in sets of five. Each new group gives a slightly different focus to what the students are doing. But the book is organized in a helical fashion so the students eventually come back to the same format of practice on a higher level.

I've been using these kinds of practices for about ten years. You'll find them easy to make if you want more and easy to modify to suit the level of your students. Each page will take approximately five minutes but there's no problem with doing less than a page or more as your time allows.

There are several things I've found helpful when I use these practices. First I try to read as naturally as possible—using reduced pronunciations like /twɛniy/ for "twenty" whenever they would occur naturally. I also avoid contrastive stress unless it's absolutely called for. Contrastive stress makes things easier to understand but if it's used in an ESL classroom situation where it wouldn't be outside of the classroom it isn't giving the students the full benefit of the practice.

As I read the practices to the students I usually walk around the room. In this way I can see how the students are doing, and they are learning to listen in all directions. Sometimes only two or three of the best students can keep up with me. Once in a while I'll continue with the problem and give those few the satisfaction of completing it. Usually I stop. I might put part of the problem on the board as I read the instructions. Or I might ask one of the better students to listen to me and put it on the board. When everybody understands what they're supposed to do I go back to the normal procedure. At the end of each problem I put the correct answer on the board.

One thing I insist on—although rarely in a one-to-one situation—is that students follow directions exactly. If they are told to move from the left-hand side of their paper to the upper right-hand corner I don't accept an answer in the middle of the paper. Perhaps once a week I find it necessary to have the students raise their left hands or point to the upper-right hand corner of the board. If this is done as a class it avoids most of the personal embarrassment. To conserve paper I usually have students draw lines to divide one sheet into four parts for practices where corners are important. Then they can think of one part as a full sheet of paper.

One last thing. Students like to do these kinds of practices on their own. So once in a while I take part of a class period, let them make up their own and try them on each other. This works best in pairs or small groups. The delivery may not be quite natural, but it does help them develop their English skills. And that's really all this book is intended to do.

This exercise will give you practice in writing letters as they are dictated. Listen carefully and write the letters as they are read. The words are all names of cities. (SUGGESTION: Pronounce the name of the city, spell it once, pronounce it again.)

1. T–O/K–Y–O

2. C– H–I/C–A/G–O

3. L–I–S/B–O–N

4. T–O/R–O–N/T–O

5. S–Y–D/N–E–Y

6. S–H–A/N–G/H–A–I

7. N–A–I/R–O/B–I

8. J–A/K–A–R/T–A

9. C–A–S–A/B–L–A–N/C–A

10. N–E–W/space/Y–O–R–K

This exercise will give you practice in writing letters as they are dictated. Listen carefully and write the letters as they are read. The words are all names of countries.

1. C–A/N–A/D–A
2. I–N/D–I–A
3. G–E–R/M–A–N–Y
4. B–R–A/Z–I–L
5. M–A/L–A–Y/S–I–A
6. R–U–S/S–I–A
7. M–E/X–I/C–O
8. P–A/K–I/S–T–A–N
9. B–E–L/G–I–U–M
10. A–U–S/T–R–A/L/I–A

This exercise will give you practice in writing letters as they are dictated. Listen carefully and write the letters as they are read. The words are all common English words.

1. R–O–P–E
2. R–O–B–E
3. F–E–A–R
4. H–E–A–R
5. L–A–C–E
6. R–A–C–E
7. M–A–I–L
8. N–A–I–L
9. B–A–S–E
10. V–A–S–E

(SUGGESTION: After you finish the listening practice have the students practice the pronunciation contrast between the pairs of words.)

This exercise will give you practice in writing letters as they are dictated. Listen carefully and write the letters as they are read. The words are all common English words.

1. M–A–K/I–N–G

2. D–R–I–V/I–N–G

3. W–R–I/T–T/E–N

4. R–I–D/I–N–G

5. H–O–P/I–N–G

6. D–R–I/V–E–N

7. W–R–I–T/I–N–G

8. L–O–V/I–N–G

9. R–U–N/N–I–N–G

10. R–I–D/D–E–N

(SUGGESTION: After you finish with the listening practice have the students practice the pronunciation contrast between 2 and 6, 7 and 3, 4 and 10. They often aren't aware of the change in vowel sound.)

This exercise will give you practice in writing letters as they are dictated. Listen carefully and write the letters as they are read. The words are all past participles of irregular verbs.

1. C–A–U/G–H–T
2. S–T–O–O–D
3. S–W–E–P–T
4. B–R–O–U/G–H–T
5. D–R–U–N–K
6. G–R–O–W–N
7. B–U–I–L–T
8. T–H–O–U/G–H–T
9. B–R–O–K–E–N
10. C–H–O–S–E–N

This exercise will give you practice in putting letters in the correct place. Listen carefully and write the letters as they are read. (NOTE: Be sure the students understand the underlined words before you begin this practice.)

1. Draw three <u>lines from left to right.</u> (Demonstrate this on the board.) On the first line put a C. On the second line put an A. On the third line put a T. What do you see?

<u>C</u> <u>A</u> <u>T</u>

2. Draw two lines <u>in a row.</u> On the second line make an E. Put an H on the first line. What word do you see?

<u>H</u> <u>E</u>

3. Make three lines in a row. On the first line write a T. On the second one put an E. On the last one write an N. What did you write?

<u>T</u> <u>E</u> <u>N</u>

4. Draw six lines from left to right. On the second line put an I. On the next line make an R. Write a C on the first line. Make an E on the last line. On the fourth line make a C. Put an L on the <u>remaining</u> line. What's the word?

<u>C</u> <u>I</u> <u>R</u> <u>C</u> <u>L</u> <u>E</u>

5. Make five lines in a row. Write an X on the second line. On the last line make an A. Put a T on the middle line. Write an R on the fourth line. Make an E on the first line. What word did you write?

<u>E</u> <u>X</u> <u>T</u> <u>R</u> <u>A</u>

This exercise will give you practice in putting letters in the correct place. Listen carefully and write the letters as they are read.

1. Draw four lines in a row. On the first line put an M. Put an L on the third line. On the next one put an E. Write an A on the remaining one. What's the word?

    <u>M</u> <u>A</u> <u>L</u> <u>E</u>

2. Draw three lines from left to right. On the last line write a P. <u>On the one before that</u> make an A. Put an R on the other line. What did you write?

    <u>R</u> <u>A</u> <u>P</u>

3. Make five <u>consecutive</u> lines. Write an E on the middle line. Put a U on the one before that. On the line <u>at the far left</u> put a G. Make a T on the last line. Write an S on the other line. (NOTE: By now you probably won't have to ask anymore what they wrote.)

    <u>G</u> <u>U</u> <u>E</u> <u>S</u> <u>T</u>

4. Make four lines in a row. Put a T on the line at the far right. On the second line write an X. Write an I on <u>the one after that.</u> On the first line write an E.

    <u>E</u> <u>X</u> <u>I</u> <u>T</u>

This exercise will give you practice in putting letters in the correct place. Listen carefully and write the letters as they are read.

1. Make five <u>horizontal</u> lines from left to right. On the fourth line put a G. Put an L on the first line. <u>After that</u> put an A. Write a U between the A and the G. On the last line make an H.

$$\underline{L} \quad \underline{A} \quad \underline{U} \quad \underline{G} \quad \underline{H}$$

2. Draw six horizontal lines. On <u>the second line from the right</u> make an I. Put an L on the line before that. On the second line from the left write a U. Put a B after it. Put a C on the line <u>to the far right</u>. Put a P on the remaining line.

$$\underline{P} \quad \underline{U} \quad \underline{B} \quad \underline{L} \quad \underline{I} \quad \underline{C}$$

3. Draw four lines. Write a P on the one at the far left. Put an I on the second line from the right. Make an A on the line between those two letters. Put an L on the last line.

$$\underline{P} \quad \underline{A} \quad \underline{I} \quad \underline{L}$$

4. Make six consecutive horizontal lines. Put an N on the third line from the left. Put a D after it. On the line at the far left make a W. On <u>the second line from the end</u> make an E. Put an O on the second line and an R on the last one.

$$\underline{W} \quad \underline{O} \quad \underline{N} \quad \underline{D} \quad \underline{E} \quad \underline{R}$$

This exercise will give you practice in putting letters in the correct place. Listen carefully and write the letters as they are read.

1. Draw four consecutive horizontal lines. Write an H on <u>the second line from the beginning</u>. Write an S <u>in front of</u> it and an I after it. Put a P on the last line.

<u>S</u>   <u>H</u>   <u>I</u>   <u>P</u>

2. Make four lines from left to right. On the second line from the right make an X. Put an I after it and an A in front of it. On the other line write a T.

<u>T</u>   <u>A</u>   <u>X</u>   <u>I</u>

3. Put four lines from left to right. On the second line write an O. Put an L after it and an E after that. Put an H on the line <u>that's left</u>.

<u>H</u>   <u>O</u>   <u>L</u>   <u>E</u>

4. Draw six horizontal lines. Put an E on the second line and an A on the fourth one. Put an M between those two letters. Write an F on the first line and an E on the last one. Make an L on the <u>blank</u> line.

<u>F</u>   <u>E</u>   <u>M</u>   <u>A</u>   <u>L</u>   <u>E</u>

This exercise will give you practice in putting letters in the correct place. Listen carefully and write the letters as they are read.

1. Draw four lines from left to right. Write a D on the first line and a T on the third one. Put an E on the last line and an A on the second one.

<u>D</u> <u>A</u> <u>T</u> <u>E</u>

2. Draw six consecutive lines. Put an H on the second and fifth lines. Write a Y after the first H and a T after that. On the line on the far left make an R. Put an M on the blank line.

<u>R</u> <u>H</u> <u>Y</u> <u>T</u> <u>H</u> <u>M</u>

3. Make three consecutive lines. Put an F on the first one, an I on the second one and an X on the third one.

<u>F</u> <u>I</u> <u>X</u>

4. Draw eight lines. Write an E on the second, fifth and last lines. Put an N after the first two E's you wrote. Make a T after the first N and a C after the second one. Put an S on the blank line.

<u>S</u> <u>E</u> <u>N</u> <u>T</u> <u>E</u> <u>N</u> <u>C</u> <u>E</u>

This exercise will give you practice in writing down whole numbers. Listen carefully and write down the numbers as they are read. Then find the answer to the problem.

.1 Write down a 7. <u>Add</u> 5. What's the answer?

$$7 + 5 = 12$$

2. Write down a 6. Add 19. What's the answer?

$$6 + 19 = 25$$

3. Write down an 8. Add 4. Add 10. What's the answer?

$$8 + 4 + 10 = 22$$

4. Write down a 9. <u>Subtract</u> 3. What's the answer?

$$9 - 3 = 6$$

5. Write down a 13. Subtract 6.

$$13 - 6 = 7$$

6. Write down a 17. Subtract 2. Subtract 5.

$$17 - 2 - 5 = 10$$

7. Write down a 15. Add 10. Subtract 20.

$$15 + 10 - 20 = 5$$

8. Write down a 33. Subtract 16. Add 13.

$$33 - 16 + 13 = 30$$

9. Write down a zero. Add 16. Subtract 15.

$$0 + 16 - 15 = 1$$

10. Write down a 28. Subtract 14. Add 19.

$$28 - 14 + 19 = 33$$

This exercise will give you practice in writing down whole numbers. Listen carefully and write down the numbers as they are read. Then find the answer to the problem.

1. Write down a 2. <u>Multiply</u> by 3. What's the answer?

$$2 \times 3 = 6$$

2. Write down a 5. Multiply by 4. What's the answer?

$$5 \times 4 = 20$$

3. Write down a 3. Multiply by 2. Multiply by 5.

$$3 \times 2 \times 5 = 30$$

4. Write down a 7. Multiply by 3. Add 4.

$$7 \times 3 + 4 = 25$$

5. Write down a 6. Add 2. Multiply by 5.

$$(6 + 2) \times 5 = 40$$

6. Write down a 10. Subtract 3. Multiply by 7.

$$(10 - 3) \times 7 = 49$$

7. Write down a 19. Add 4. Multiply by 2.

$$(19 + 4) \times 2 = 46$$

8. Write down a 5. Multiply by 3. Subtract 8.

$$5 \times 3 - 8 = 7$$

9. Write down a 15. Multiply by 3. Add 10.

$$15 \times 3 + 10 = 55$$

10. Write down a 27. Subtract 12. Multiply by 4.

$$(27 - 12) \times 4 = 60$$

This exercise will give you practice in writing down whole numbers. Listen carefully and write down the numbers as they are read. Then find the answer to the problem.

1. Write down an 8. <u>Divide</u> by 4. What's the answer?

$$8 \div 4 = 2$$

2. Write down a 27. Divide by 3.

$$27 \div 3 = 9$$

3. Write down a 36. Divide by 4. Divide by 3.

$$36 \div 4 \div 3 = 3$$

4. Write down a 25. <u>Divide</u> 5 <u>into</u> it.

$$25 \div 5 = 5$$

5. Write down a 17. Add 13. Divide 3 into that.

$$(17 + 13) \div 3 = 10$$

6. Write down a 15. Add 7. Divide by 2.

$$(15 + 7) \div 2 = 11$$

7. Write down a 70. Subtract 16. Divide by 9.

$$(70 - 16) \div 9 = 6$$

8. Write down an 18. Divide by 6. Add 30.

$$18 \div 6 + 30 = 33$$

9. Write down a 50. Subtract 2. Divide by 6. Add 17.

$$(50 - 2) \div 6 + 17 = 25$$

This exercise will give you practice in writing down whole numbers. Listen carefully and write down the numbers as they are read. Then find the answer to the problem.

1. Write down a 16. Divide by 4. Multiply by 5.

$$16 \div 4 \times 5 = 20$$

2. Write down a 40. Add 5. Divide by 9.

$$(40 + 5) \div 9 = 5$$

3. Write down a 13. Multiply by 5. Subtract 4.

$$13 \times 5 - 4 = 61$$

4. Write down a 35. Divide by 7. Multiply by 8.

$$35 \div 7 \times 8 = 40$$

5. Write down an 80. Divide by 16. Multiply by 9.

$$80 \div 16 \times 9 = 45$$

6. Write down a 27. Add 3. Multiply by 4.

$$(27 + 3) \times 4 = 120$$

7. Write down a 15. Add 60. Divide by 5.

$$(15 + 60) \div 5 = 15$$

8. Write down a 100. Divide by 20. Multiply by 10.

$$100 \div 20 \times 10 = 50$$

9. Write down a 70. Multiply by 5. Divide by 50.

$$70 \times 5 \div 50 = 7$$

10. Write down a 63. Divide by 9. Add 6. Multiply by 5. Subtract 30.

$$(63 \div 9)(+6) \times 5 - 30 = 35$$

This exercise will give you practice in writing down whole numbers. Listen carefully and write down the numbers as they are read. Then find the answer to the problem.

1. Write down a 9. <u>Find the square root.</u> Add 7.

$$\sqrt{9} = 3 + 7 = 10$$

2. Write down a 25. Find the square root. Subtract 2.

$$\sqrt{25} = 5 - 2 = 3$$

3. Write down a 30. Add 19. Find the square root.

$$30 + 19 = \sqrt{49} = 7$$

4. Write down a 4. <u>Square it.</u> Subtract 7.

$$4^2 = 16 - 7 = 9$$

5. Write down an 8. Square it. Add 16.

$$8^2 = 64 + 16 = 80$$

6. Write down a 9. Square it. Subtract 17.

$$9^2 = 81 - 17 = 64$$

7. Write down a 13. Add 3. Find the square root. Multiply by 14.

$$13 + 3 = \sqrt{16} = 4 \times 14 = 56$$

8. Write down a 60. Divide by 3. Subtract 10. Square that number.

$$60 \div 3 = 20 - 10 = 10^2 = 100$$

9. Write down a 36. Find the square root. Multiply by 18. Subtract 50.

$$\sqrt{36} = 6 \times 18 - 50 = 58$$

This exercise will give you practice in putting numbers and letters in the correct place. Listen carefully and write them as they are read.

1. Draw a horizontal line. Put a 6 <u>under</u> it.

$$\frac{}{6}$$

2. Draw a horizontal line. Put a 3 under it. Make a 7 above it.

$$\frac{7}{3}$$

3. Make two horizontal lines in a row. Put a 2 <u>beneath</u> the first one. Put an E above the second one.

$$\frac{}{2} \quad \overset{E}{\overline{}}$$

4. Draw two consecutive horizontal lines. Put a 2 <u>over</u> the second one. Put a 9 under the same line.

$$\overline{} \quad \frac{2}{9}$$

5. Make two horizontal lines. Put a T <u>below</u> the first one and a 13 over the second one.

$$\underset{T}{\overline{}} \quad \overset{13}{\overline{}}$$

6. Make two horizontal lines. Put a 14 under the first one and a 40 beneath the other one.

$$\overline{14} \quad \overline{40}$$

7. Draw three consecutive horizontal lines. Put a 16 over the first one and an X beneath the third one. Write a 28 under the other one.

$$\frac{16}{} \quad \frac{}{28} \quad \underset{X}{\overline{}}$$

This exercise will give you practice putting numbers and letters in the correct place. Listen carefully and write them as they are read.

1. Draw a <u>vertical</u> line. Put a 16 <u>to the left of</u>it.   16 |

2. Make a vertical line. Write a 75 <u>on the right of</u> it. | 75

3. Draw a vertical line. Write a 60 beneath it. Put a B to the right of it.

        | B
        60

4. Make a vertical line. Make a 17 above it and a 14 to the right of it.

        17
        | 14

5. Draw two <u>parallel</u> vertical lines. Put an 18 between them. | 18 |

6. Make two parallel vertical lines. Put a 48 to the left of them. Put a 19 to the right of them. Add the numbers and put the answer between the lines.   48 | 67 | 19

7. Draw two parallel vertical lines. Put a 35 to the right of them. Put a 7 between them. Subtract the smaller number from the bigger one and put your answer to the left of the lines.   28 | 7 | 35

This exercise will give you practice putting numbers and letters in the correct place. Listen carefully and write them as they are read.

1. Draw a <u>diagonal</u> line. Put a 12 to the left of it. Make a 40 to the right of it.

    Accept   12\\40   OR   12/40

2. Make a diagonal line. Write a 17 to the right of it and a 28 to the left of it.

    Accept   28\\17   OR   28/17

3. Draw a diagonal line <u>from the top left to the bottom right.</u> Put a G under it. Make a 92 above it.

    G\\92

4. Make a diagonal line from the top right to the bottom left. Put an S over it and an X below it.

    S/X

5. Draw two parallel diagonal lines from the top left to the bottom right. Put a 13 between them. Put an A beneath them.

    A\\13\\

6. Draw three parallel diagonal lines from the top right to the bottom left. Put a 15 between the bottom two. Write a 70 above the top one.

    70/ /15/

This exercise will give you practice putting numbers and letters in the correct place. Listen carefully and write them as they are read.

1. Draw three consecutive horizontal lines. Put a 60 over the first one and an S beneath the second one. Write a 28 above the other one.

    $$\underline{60} \quad \underset{S}{\underline{}} \quad \underline{28}$$

2. Draw two parallel vertical lines. Put a 48 to the left of them. Put a 19 to the right of them. Add the numbers and put the answer between the lines.

    $$48 | 67 | 19$$

3. Make three horizontal lines from left to right. Put a 5 below the first one, a 7 above the second one and an A under the third one.

    $$\underset{5}{\underline{}} \quad \overset{7}{\underline{}} \quad \underset{A}{\underline{}}$$

4. Draw <u>a pair</u> of vertical parallel lines. Put a 48 to the right of them and a 6 between them. Divide the smaller number into the bigger one and put your answer to the left of the lines.

    $$8 | 6 | 48$$

5. Draw three parallel diagonal lines <u>in any direction.</u> Write a 16 between the top two. Make a 36 beneath the bottom one. Find the square root of the smaller number and write your answer between the bottom two lines.

    Accept   16   OR   16
                  4   4
              36   36

This exercise will give you practice putting numbers and letters in the correct place. Listen carefully and write them as they are read.

1. <u>Working from left to right</u> draw a horizontal line, a vertical line and a diagonal line from the top left to the bottom right. Put an F on the horizontal line.

$$\underline{F} \mid \diagdown$$

2. <u>Starting on the right</u> make a vertical line and two horizontal lines. Write a 24 on the middle line.

$$\_\_ \quad \underline{24} \quad \mid$$

3. Starting on the left draw a vertical line and a horizontal line. Then draw two diagonal lines that <u>intersect</u>. Put an 8 to the right of the vertical line and an H on the horizontal line.

$$\mid 8 \, \underline{H} \quad \times$$

4. Make a pair of parallel vertical lines <u>followed by</u> two horizontal lines. Write a 15 between the vertical lines and a D on the second horizontal line.

$$\mid 15 \mid \_\_ \quad \underline{D}$$

5. Draw a horizontal line, a vertical line and another horizontal line. Put a 17 on the second horizontal line followed by a diagonal line from the top left to the bottom right.

$$\_\_ \mid \underline{17} \diagdown$$

This exercise will give you practice putting numbers and letters in the correct place. Listen carefully and write them as they are read.

1. Draw a <u>circle.</u> Put an H <u>inside of</u> it.

2. Draw a <u>square.</u> Write a 19 to the left of it.

3. Make a circle. Put a 50 inside of it and a 13 to the left of it.

4. Draw a <u>triangle</u> with the <u>apex</u> at the bottom. Write a 78 beneath the <u>base.</u>

5. Make a square. Put a 14 to the left of it. Write a 5 above it.

6. Draw a triangle. Make a square inside of the triangle.

7. Make a <u>rectangle.</u> Draw a circle around it.

8. Make a triangle with the apex <u>pointing down.</u> Draw a square around it and put a 15 inside of it.

This exercise will give you practice putting numbers and letters in the correct place. Listen carefully and write them as they are read.

1. Draw two squares <u>next to each other</u>. Write a G in between them.

2. Make two circles, <u>one above the other</u>. Put a 17 in the top one.

3. Draw a triangle. Make a circle to the left of it. Draw a vertical line between them.

4. Draw two triangles next to each other. Make a horizontal line in the <u>right-hand</u> one.

5. Draw a pair of circles, one above the other. Write an E in the bottom one.

6. Working from left to right make a circle, a rectangle and a triangle. Put a 28 in the left-hand <u>figure</u> you drew.

This exercise will give you practice putting numbers and letters in the correct place. Listen carefully and write them as they are read.

1. Draw two squares, one below the other. Put a 17 in the <u>upper</u> one.

2. Make three triangles from left to right. Put an F in the left-hand one and an H in the right-hand one.

3. Draw a pair of circles, one below the other. Write an 8 in the <u>lower</u> one.

4. Make two consecutive rectangles. Put a diagonal line from the top right to the bottom left in the right-hand one.

5. Draw two consecutive triangles. Put a circle around the left-hand triangle and a 15 inside of it.

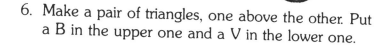

6. Make a pair of triangles, one above the other. Put a B in the upper one and a V in the lower one.

7. Starting at the right draw a circle, a square, another circle and a triangle. Write a C in the right-hand circle.

This exercise will give you practice in putting numbers and letters in the correct place. Listen carefully and write them as they are read.

1. Draw a circle. <u>Bisect</u> it from left to right. Put an A in the upper <u>half</u>

2. Draw a square. Bisect if from top to bottom. Write a 50 in the left-hand part.

3. Draw a circle. Bisect if from top to bottom and left to right. Put a 6 in the upper left-hand <u>sector.</u>

4. Draw a square. Divide it into four <u>equal</u> smaller squares. Make a Z in the lower right-hand square.

5. Make a rectangle. Divide it in half from left to right. In the upper half draw a triangle with the apex pointing down.

6. Draw a circle. Bisect it from top to bottom and left to right. Put a 13 in the upper right-hand sector and a 5 in the upper left-hand sector.

This exercise will give you practice in putting numbers and letters in the correct place. Listen carefully and write them as they are read.

1. Draw a circle. Bisect it from top to bottom and left to right. Put a 6 in the upper right-hand sector. Write a U in the lower left-hand sector.

2. Draw a triangle. Make a circle around it. Put a 40 between the left-hand side of the triangle and the circle.

3. Make a square. Divide it into four equal smaller squares. Write an S in the lower left-hand square. Put an X in the one <u>directly</u> above that.

4. Draw a square. Make a triangle around it. Put a 28 between the square and the apex of the triangle.

5. Draw two squares next to each other. Divide them in half from left to right. Put a circle in the lower half of the right-hand one.

6. Draw a circle. Bisect it from top to bottom and from left to right. Put a 39 in the upper right-hand sector. Write a G in the sector that's <u>diagonally opposite</u>.

This exercise will give you practice in writing words in the correct place. Listen carefully and follow the directions.

1. Draw a vertical line. To the left of it write this word: W–O–N. To the right of it write this word: O–N–E.

   WON | ONE

2. Draw a horizontal line. Above it write this word: P–A–I–R. Below it write this word: P–A–R–E.

   PAIR
   ‾‾‾‾‾
   PARE

3. Make a rectangle. Inside of it write this word: M–A–I–L. Below it write this word: M–A–L–E.

   MAIL
   MALE

4. Make a big circle. Inside of it write this word: R–I/G–H–T. Write this word — W–R–I/T–E — to the right of it.

   RIGHT WRITE

5. Draw a diagonal line from the top left to the bottom right. Above it write this word: N–I/G–H–T. Write this word — K–N–I/G–H–T — beneath it.

   NIGHT
   KNIGHT

(SUGGESTION: After you finish the listening practice have the students practice the pronunciation of the words.)

This exercise will give you practice in writing words in the correct place. Listen carefully and follow the directions.

1. Draw a pair of circles. Writing from top to bottom between the circles write this word: R–E–B/E–L.

2. Draw a pair of parallel horizontal lines. Between them write this word: C–O–N/D–U–C–T.

3. Make two rectangles, one above the other. In the lower one write this word: I–N/C–R–E/A–S–E.

4. Draw a square followed by a circle. Write this word — S–U–S/P–E–C–T — in the circle.

5. Draw a pair of parallel diagonal lines from the top left to the bottom right. Write this word between them: R–E/C–O–R–D.

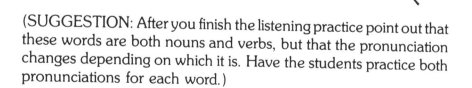

(SUGGESTION: After you finish the listening practice point out that these words are both nouns and verbs, but that the pronunciation changes depending on which it is. Have the students practice both pronunciations for each word.)

This exercise will give you practice in writing words in the correct place. Listen carefully and follow the directions.

1. Write this word: G–E–T/T–I–N–G. To the right of it write this word: M–E–E–T/I––N–G. Now draw an <u>oval</u> around the word that has a <u>double</u> T.

   <u>(GETTING)</u>   MEETING

2. Write this word: S–W–I–M/M–I–N–G. Below it write this word: F–A–R–M/E–R. Now <u>underline</u> the word that's got a <u>single</u> M.

   SWIMMING
   <u>FARMER</u>

3. Write this word: M–O–O–N. Right after it write this word: C–O–U/G–H. Now draw an oval around the word that has a double vowel.

   (MOON)   COUGH

4. Write this word: O–C–C/U–P–Y. Above it write this word: S–A–I–L/E–D. Now make a rectangle around the word that has a double consonant.

   SAILED
   [OCCUPY]

5. Write this word: S–T–A–R–T/I––N–G. To the right of it write this word: C–U–T–T–I–N–G. Underline the word that has a double T.

   STARTING   <u>CUTTING</u>

This exercise will give you practice in writing words in the correct place. Listen carefully and follow the directions.

1. Write this word: O–V–E–N. Beneath it write this word: B–O–A–T. Draw a rectangle around the word that has an /o/ sound.

oven

boat

2. Write this word: C–O–U–S–I–N. Above it write this word: H–O–U–S–E. Put a <u>check</u> to the right of the one that has an /au/ sound.

house ✓

cousin

3. Write this word: B–E–A–T. To the right of it write this word: B–I–T. Underline the word that has an /ē/ sound.

<u>*beat*</u> *bit*

4. Write this word: B–A–R–K. Under it write this word: P–A–R–K. Make an oval around the word that doesn't have a P in it.

bark

park

5. Draw a circle. To the left of it write this word: P–O–O–L. Below it write this word: P–U–L–L. Draw another circle around the word that doesn't have an /oo/ sound in it.

pool

pull

This exercise will give you practice in writing words in the correct place. Listen carefully and follow the directions.

1. Write this word: S–H–A–P–E. Next to it write this word: M–A–L–E. Now add a D to the word that can be a verb.

   shaped   male

2. Write this word: P–L–A–C–E. Below it write this word: A–S–K. Now add an S to the word that can be either a verb or a noun.

   places
   ask

3. Write this word: W–E–I–G–H–T. Above it write this word: T–A–U–G–H–T. Now to the right of these words write the present tense form of the verb.

   taught
   weight   teach

4. Write this word: F–O–O–D. Next to it make a square. Under the square write this word: R–I–D–E. Now in the square write the past tense form of the verb.

   food |rode|
   ride

5. Make a circle. To the left of it write C–A–R and to the right of it write B–I–K–E. Add an S to the word that can be either a noun or a verb.

   car ◯ bikes

This exercise will give you practice in writing down <u>fractions.</u> Listen carefully and write down the numbers as they are read.

1. Draw a circle. Put the fraction ¹/₃ in it.

2. Make a square. Write the fraction ²/₅ above it.

3. Draw a vertical line. To the right of it write the fraction ³/₄.

4. Make a horizontal line. Put the fraction ⁷/₈ beneath it.

5. Make a pair of parallel vertical lines. Write the fraction ¹¹/₁₂ between them.

6. Draw two circles, one above the other. Put the fraction ⁹/₁₆ in the lower one.

7. Make a square followed by a triangle. Write the fraction ¹⁷/₃₂ in the triangle.

   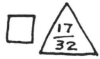

This exercise will give you practice in writing down fractions. Listen carefully and write the numbers as they are read.

1. Write down $^1/_2$. Multiply by 4. What's the answer?

$$\frac{1}{2} \times 4 = 2$$

2. Write down $^2/_3$. Add 5. What's the answer?

$$\frac{2}{3} + 5 = 5\frac{2}{3}$$

3. Write down $^3/_4$. Multiply by 4. What's the answer?

$$\frac{3}{4} \times 4 = 3$$

4. Write down $^7/_8$. Add 16.

$$\frac{7}{8} + 16 = 16\frac{7}{8}$$

5. Write down $^5/_{16}$. Multiply by 3.

$$\frac{5}{16} \times 3 = \frac{15}{16}$$

6. Write down a 15. Multiply by $^1/_3$.

$$15 \times \frac{1}{3} = 5$$

7. Write down a 70. Add $^{13}/_{17}$.

$$70 + \frac{13}{17} = 70\frac{13}{17}$$

8. Write down a 40. Multiply by $^3/_4$.

$$40 \times \frac{3}{4} = 30$$

9. Write down $^4/_9$. Multiply by 2.

$$\frac{4}{9} \times 2 = \frac{8}{9}$$

10. Write down $^{15}/_{32}$. Add $^{14}/_{32}$.

$$\frac{15}{32} + \frac{14}{32} = \frac{29}{32}$$

This exercise will give you practice in writing down fractions. Listen carefully and write the numbers as they are read.

1. Write down $1/2$. Add $3/2$. Change your answer to a whole number.

$$\frac{1}{2} + \frac{3}{2} = \frac{4}{2} = 2$$

2. Write down $1/3$. Add $8/3$. Change your answer to a whole number.

$$\frac{1}{3} + \frac{8}{3} = \frac{9}{3} = 3$$

3. Write down $3/5$. Add $7/5$. Change your answer to a whole number.

$$\frac{3}{5} + \frac{7}{5} = \frac{10}{5} = 2$$

4. Write down $4/3$. Multiply by 3. Change your answer to a whole number.

$$\frac{4}{3} \times 3 = \frac{12}{3} = 4$$

5. Write down $5/4$. Multiply by 4. Change your answer to a whole number.

$$\frac{5}{4} \times 4 = \frac{20}{4} = 5$$

6. Write down $1/6$. Multiply by 2. <u>Reduce</u> your answer.

$$\frac{1}{6} \times 2 = \frac{2}{6} = \frac{1}{3}$$

7. Write down $9/16$. Add $7/16$. Change your answer to a whole number.

$$\frac{9}{16} + \frac{7}{16} = \frac{16}{16} = 1$$

8. Write down $5/12$. Multiply by 2. Reduce your answer.

$$\frac{5}{12} \times 2 = \frac{10}{12} = \frac{5}{6}$$

9. Write down $17/32$. Add $7/32$. Reduce your answer.

$$\frac{17}{32} + \frac{7}{32} = \frac{24}{32} = \frac{3}{4}$$

10. Write down $4/9$. Add $2 5/9$. Change your answer to a whole number.

$$\frac{4}{9} + 2\frac{5}{9} = 2\frac{9}{9} = 3$$

This exercise will give you practice in writing down fractions. Listen carefully and write the numbers as they are read.

1. Write down $^1/_2$. Add 15. Subtract $1^1/_2$.

$$\frac{1}{2} + 15 - 1\frac{1}{2} = 14$$

2. Write down $^3/_4$. Add 70. Subtract $2\,^3/_4$.

$$\frac{3}{4} + 70 - 2\frac{3}{4} = 68$$

3. Write down $^9/_{16}$. Add 14. Subtract $^7/_{16}$. Reduce your answer.

$$\frac{9}{16} + 14 - \frac{7}{16} = 14\frac{2}{16} = 14\frac{1}{8}$$

4. Write down $5\,^5/_9$. Subtract $2\,^4/_9$.

$$5\frac{5}{9} - 2\frac{4}{9} = 3\frac{1}{9}$$

5. Write down $8\,^3/_4$. Subtract $2\,^1/_4$. Add 3. Reduce your answer.

$$8\frac{3}{4} - 2\frac{1}{4} + 3 = 9\frac{2}{4} = 9\frac{1}{2}$$

6. Write down $^{19}/_{32}$. Add $^{17}/_{32}$. Subtract $^{15}/_{32}$.

$$\frac{19}{32} + \frac{17}{32} - \frac{15}{32} = \frac{21}{32}$$

7. Write down $8\,^4/_5$. Multiply by 2. Subtract $^4/_5$.

$$8\frac{4}{5} \times 2 - \frac{4}{5} = 16\frac{4}{5}$$

8. Write down $15\,^{31}/_{64}$. Subtract $9\,^{16}/_{64}$. Multiply by 3.

$$15\frac{31}{64} - 9\frac{16}{64} \times 3 = 18\frac{45}{64}$$

This exercise will give you practice in writing down fractions. Listen carefully and write the numbers as they are read.

1. Write down the fractions $1/3$ and $4/3$. Add them together. Change your answer to <u>a mixed fraction.</u> $\frac{1}{3} + \frac{4}{3} = \frac{5}{3} = 1\frac{2}{3}$

2. Write down the fractions $1/6$ and $7/6$. Add them together. Change your answer to a mixed fraction.

   $$\frac{1}{6} + \frac{7}{6} = \frac{8}{6} = 1\frac{2}{6} = 1\frac{1}{3}$$

3. Write down the fractions $3/11$ and $10/11$. Add them together. Change your answer to a mixed fraction.

   $$\frac{3}{11} + \frac{10}{11} = \frac{13}{11} = 1\frac{2}{11}$$

4. Write down $13/16$ and $15/16$. Add them together. Change your answer to a mixed fraction. $\frac{13}{16} + \frac{15}{16} = \frac{28}{16} = 1\frac{12}{16} = 1\frac{3}{4}$

5. Write down $15/32$ and $13/32$. Subtract the second fraction from the first one. Reduce your answer. $\frac{15}{32} - \frac{13}{32} = \frac{2}{32} = \frac{1}{16}$

6. Write down $19/64$ and $47/64$. Subtract the first fraction from the second one. Reduce your answer. $\frac{47}{64} - \frac{19}{64} = \frac{28}{64} = \frac{7}{16}$

7. Write down $5/19$ and $13/19$. Subtract the smaller one from the larger one. $\frac{13}{19} - \frac{5}{19} = \frac{8}{19}$

8. Write down $19/32$ and $15/32$. Subtract the smaller one from the larger one. Reduce your answer.

   $$\frac{19}{32} - \frac{15}{32} = \frac{4}{32} = \frac{1}{8}$$

This exercise will give you practice in putting <u>shapes</u> in the correct place. Listen carefully and follow the instructions.

1. Draw a circle. Above the circle make a triangle. Put a square to the right of the triangle.

2. Make a triangle. Draw a circle to the left of it. Put a square under the circle.

3. Draw a pair of circles, one after the other. Put a square above the right-hand one. Put a triangle beneath the other one.

4. Make three squares in a row. Put a circle above the middle one. To the left of the circle draw a triangle.

This exercise will give you practice in putting shapes in the correct place. Listen carefully and follow the instructions. (SUGGESTION: After you finish Number 4 you might want to emphasize the difference in meaning between "to the left of IT" in Number 2 and "to the left of THAT" in Number 3.)

1. Draw a square. Below the square make a triangle. To the right of the triangle make a circle. Put an X in the triangle.

2. Draw a triangle. To the left of it draw a square. Below it draw another square. Put an 8 in the triangle.

3. Draw a circle. Above it draw a triangle. To the left of that make a square. Put an H in the square.

4. Make a circle. Beneath it draw a triangle. To the right of the triangle make a square. Put an S in the circle.

This exercise will give you practice in getting shapes in the correct place. Listen carefully and follow the instructions.

1. Make a triangle. Draw a circle on both sides of it. Put a 15 in the left-hand circle.

2. Draw a circle followed by a rectangle. Put a 40 in the rectangle and a triangle above the circle.

3. Make a square with a circle inside of it. Write a V inside the circle and a B to the right of the square.

4. Make a circle. Put a square on each side of it. Draw a circle below the right-hand square. Put an 80 in the lower circle.

   This exercise will give you practice in putting shapes in the correct place. Listen carefully and follow the instructions.

1. Draw a square with a circle around it. Put a 6 between the top of the square and the circle. Make an S below the circle.

2. Make a triangle followed by two circles. Put a 19 in the left-hand circle and an H in the triangle.

3. Draw a circle with a rectangle to the left of it. Put a triangle with a 30 in it below the circle.

4. Make two circles with a triangle between them. Put a triangle beneath the right-hand circle. Write a G in the upper triangle.

This exercise will give you practice in putting shapes in the correct place. Listen carefully and follow the instructions.

1. Make a circle and a square with a triangle between them. Put a 50 in the circle and a 25 in the square. Draw a diagonal line from the apex of the triangle to the lower left-hand corner of the square.

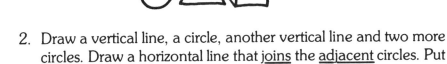

2. Draw a vertical line, a circle, another vertical line and two more circles. Draw a horizontal line that <u>joins</u> the <u>adjacent</u> circles. Put an M under it.

3. Draw a circle with a rectangle above it. To the right of the rectangle make a circle with a rectangle below it. Put a circle beneath the lower rectangle. Write an 18 in the middle circle and a 23 in the lower one. Put an F in the upper rectangle and an H in the other circle.

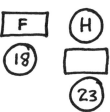

This exercise will give you practice working with whole numbers. Listen carefully and follow the instructions.

1. From left to right write a 16, a 90 and a 23. Draw an oval around the biggest number.   16 (90) 23

2. From right to left write a 13, a 5, a 28 and a 60. Put a square around the smallest number.   60 28 [5] 13

3. From top to bottom write the numbers from 1 to 5. Put a circle around the second number from the top. Put a triangle around the third number from the bottom.

    1
    ②
    △3△
    4
    5

4. Working from left to right write these numbers: 4–9–7–21–5. Underline the middle number.

    4 9 7 21 5

5. Working <u>from the top down</u> write the numbers 14–30–16–90–20. Draw a horizontal line between the smallest number and the number below it.

    14
    ——
    30
    16
    90
    20

   This exercise will give you practice working with whole numbers. Listen carefully and follow the instructions.

1. Draw four consecutive horizontal lines. On the first line put a 16. On the second one put a 5. Add the numbers together. Put your answer on the last line.

$$\underline{16}\ \underline{5}\ \underline{\quad}\ \underline{21}$$

2. Make five consecutive horizontal lines. On the second one from the end put a 32. On the line before that put a 19. Add the numbers together. Put your answer on the line after the 32.

$$\underline{\quad}\ \underline{\quad}\ \underline{19}\ \underline{32}\ \underline{51}$$

3. Make the same number of lines as you did in the last problem. On the second line from the beginning write a 92. Put a 41 on the last line. Subtract the smaller number from the bigger one. Put your answer on the middle line.

$$\underline{\quad}\ \underline{92}\ \underline{51}\ \underline{\quad}\ \underline{41}$$

4. Draw six consecutive horizontal lines. Write an 80 on the first line and a 16 on the last one. Subtract the smaller number from the bigger one. Put your answer on the third line from the end.

$$\underline{80}\ \underline{\quad}\ \underline{\quad}\ \underline{64}\ \underline{\quad}\ \underline{16}$$

This exercise will give you practice working with whole numbers. Listen carefully and follow the instructions.

1. Draw four consecutive horizontal lines. Write a 75 on the first line. Put a 15 on the last one. Divide the smaller number into the bigger one. Put your answer on the second line.

$$\underline{75}\ \underline{5}\ \underline{\ \ }\ \underline{15}$$

2. Make four consecutive horizontal lines. Put a 7 on the third line and a 5 on the first one. Multiply the numbers. Put your answer between the numbers you already wrote.

$$\underline{5}\ \underline{35}\ \underline{7}\ \underline{\ \ }$$

3. Make five parallel horizontal lines. On the top line put a 48. Write a 6 on the second line from the bottom. Divide the larger number by the smaller one. Put your answer on the lower line.

$$\underline{48}$$
$$\underline{}$$
$$\underline{}$$
$$\underline{6}$$
$$\underline{8}$$

4. Draw three consecutive horizontal lines. On the left-hand line put a 14 and write a 3 on the last one. Multiply the numbers and put your answer on the blank line.

$$\underline{14}\ \underline{42}\ \underline{3}$$

This exercise will give you practice working with whole numbers. Listen carefully and follow the instructions.

1. Draw four parallel horizontal lines. Write a 5 on the top one. Put a 7 on the second one. Put an 8 on the bottom one. Square the smallest number. Put your answer on the blank line.

    $$\frac{5}{7}$$
    $$\frac{}{25}$$
    $$\frac{}{8}$$

2. Draw four consecutive horizontal lines. On the first line write a 49. Put a 64 on the second line from the end. On the line between those two numbers write a 100. Find the square root of the biggest number and put your answer on the remaining line.

    49 100 64 10

3. Draw five parallel vertical lines. Put an A between the first two lines. Write a 6 between the last two. Put a 3 between the two lines before the 6. Square the largest number and write your answer after the last line.

    |A| |3|6|36

This exercise will give you practice working with whole numbers. Listen carefully and follow the instructions.

1. Draw four consecutive horizontal lines. Starting from the left put a 6, an 8 and a 23 on the first three lines. Subtract the two smallest numbers from the biggest one and write your answer on the remaining line.

    <u>6</u> <u>8</u> <u>23</u> <u>9</u>

2. Beginning at the left make a circle, a vertical line, a triangle and a horizontal line. Write an 18 in the circle and the triangle. Put a 50 on the horizontal line. Add all the nubers together and put your answer between the circle and the vertical line.

3. Draw three parallel vertical lines followed by three consecutive horizontal lines. Put a 5 between the first two lines. Put a 16 on the fourth line from the beginning. Add the two numbers together and put your answer in the <u>space</u> between the last two vertical lines.

    |5|21| <u>16</u> <u> </u> <u> </u>

This exercise will give you practice writing words. Listen carefully and follow the instructions.

1. Write this word: L–E–I–S–U–R–E. To the right of it write this word: S–I–Z–E. Draw an oval around the word that has an S sound in it.

LEISURE   (SIZE)

2. Write this word: L–A–U–G–H. Write this word beneath it: W–E–I–G–H–T. Put a check to the left of the word in which GH isn't pronounced.

LAUGH
✔WEIGHT

3. Write this word: R–E–A–D. Above it write this word: S–H–A–P–E–D. Draw a rectangle around the word in which the D is pronounced like a T.

[SHAPED]
READ

This exercise will give you practice writing letters. Listen carefully and follow the directions.

1. Make eight consecutive horizontal lines. Beginning with the first line write one of these letters on <u>alternate</u> lines: A–G–N–T. Now put the letter that comes after each of those letters in the alphabet.

    <u>A</u> <u>B</u> <u>G</u> <u>H</u> <u>N</u> <u>O</u><u>T</u> <u>U</u>

2. Make eight consecutive horizontal lines. Beginning with the second line write one of these letters on alternate lines: E–Z–J–V. Now put the letter that comes before each of those letters in the alphabet.

    <u>D</u> <u>E</u> <u>Y</u> <u>Z</u> <u>I</u> <u>J</u> <u>U</u> <u>V</u>

3. Make eight consecutive horizontal lines. Beginning with the first line and using <u>every other line</u> write one of these letters: M–K–Y–X. For the first two letters write the letters that come after them and for the last one the letter that comes before it.

    <u>M</u> <u>N</u> <u>K</u> <u>L</u> <u>Y</u> <u>W</u><u>X</u> <u>_</u>

   This exercise will give you practice writing letters. Listen carefully and follow the directions.

1. Draw six consecutive horizontal lines. Starting at the left write these letters: S–C/skip a line/O–O–L. What letter goes in the blank?

   S C (H) O O L

2. Draw six consecutive horizontal lines. Starting at the left write these letters: C–O/skip a line/F/skip a line/E. What letters go in the blanks?

   C O (F) F (E) E

3. Draw eight parallel horizontal lines. Starting at the top write these letters: P–R/skip a line/C/skip two lines/C–E. Can you figure out which letters are missing?

P
R
(A)
C
(T)
(I)
C
E

This exercise will give you practice writing words. Listen carefully and follow the directions.

1. Write down these words: M–A–N–S/P–I–N–K/J–A–I–L. Underline the one that's <u>spelled incorrectly</u>.

<u>MANS</u>   PINK   JAIL

2. Write down these three words: S–I–M–C–E/M–A–U–T–H/ F–A–R–M–S. Make a check over the one that's spelled correctly

SIMCE   MAUTH   ✔FARMS

3. Write down these four words: W–A–R–M/S–I–N–G/W–I–N–D /P–A–I–L. Circle the word that can be an adjective.

(WARM)   SING   WIND   PAIL

This exercise will give you practice writing letters. The words used in this practice are the names of cities. But the names have been <u>scrambled</u>. (SUGGESTION: You might want to use your own name to explain the meaning of this word.) Listen carefully and follow the directions.

1. Make a rectangle. Inside of it write these letters: R–I–P–S–A. Now unscramble the name and write it above the rectangle.

2. Draw an oval. To the right of it write these letters: M–O–R–E. Now unscramble the name and write it inside the oval.

3. Draw a vertical line. To the right of it write these letters: P–I–G–K–E–N. Now unscramble the name and write it on the other side of the line.

PEKING|PIGKEN

4. Make two rectangles. Divide them from left to right. In the lower half of the left-hand one write these letters: A–C–C–H–I–O–G. Now unscramble the name and write it in the upper half of the right-hand rectangle.

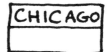

This exercise will give you practice putting figures in the right place. Follow the directions carefully.

1. Draw a circle with a 5-centimeter <u>diameter.</u> (SUGGESTION: Explain to the students that they don't actually have to measure. The numbers are only to give them an idea of relative size. Some will still want to measure though.) To the right of it draw a circle with a 3-centimeter diameter.

2. Draw a square with a 4-centimeter <u>base.</u> Beneath that make a circle with a 5-centimeter diameter. Put a check in the bigger figure.

3. Draw two circles <u>side by side</u> with 5-centimeter diameters. Join them in the middle with a horizontal line.

4. Make two squares one above the other. Make the bottom one 5 centimeters and the top one 4 centimeters. Divide the top one with a vertical line.

This exercise will give you practice putting figures in the right place. Follow the directions carefully.

1. Make a triangle with a 5-centimeter base and a <u>height</u> of 4 centimeters. To the left of it draw a circle with a 3-centimeter diameter.

2. Draw a rectangle. The top and bottom should be 5-centimeters. The sides should be 3-centimeters. Make a circle inside of it.

3. Make a circle with a 6-centimeter diameter. Make a triangle to the right of it. The height should be 4 centimeters and the base 3 centimeters. Put an H in the smaller figure.

4. Draw a square with a 6-centimeter base. Inside of it draw a circle with a 4-centimeter diameter. Write an S between the <u>perimeter</u> of the circle and the upper right-hand corner of the square.

This exercise will give you practice putting figures in the right place. Follow the directions carefully.

1. Draw a square with a 5-centimeter base. Draw a diagonal line from the upper left-hand corner to the lower right-hand corner. Write a 60 in the upper half.

2. Make a triangle with a 4-centimeter base and a 6-centimeter height. Draw a circle with a 5-centimeter diameter that touches the apex of the triangle.

3. Make a rectangle with a 5-centimeter base and 6-centimeter sides. Bisect it with a vertical line. Write a T in the left-hand part.

4. Draw a circle followed by a square with 5-centimeter <u>dimensions.</u> Connect the circle to the lower left-hand corner of the square with a horizontal line.

This exercise will give you practice putting figures and lines in the right place. Follow the directions carefully.

1. Draw a 4-centimeter horizontal line. From the right-hand end of the line draw a 5-centimeter diagonal line that goes up and to the right.

2. Make a 6-centimeter horizontal line. From the left-hand end of the line draw a 4-centimeter diagonal line that goes down and to the right. Put a V in the <u>angle.</u>

3. Make a 4-centimeter vertical line. From the top of it draw a 5-centimeter diagonal line that goes down to the right. Draw a circle around this figure.

4. Draw a 5-centimeter diagonal line from the top left to the bottom right. Draw a 3-centimeter horizontal line that bisects the diagonal line. Write an F in the upper right-hand angle.

This exercise will give you practice putting lines in the right place. Follow the directions carefully.

1. Draw a 4-centimeter line from left to right. From the middle of that line draw a 5-centimeter <u>perpendicular</u> line down.

T

2. Draw a 4-centimeter vertical line. Move 3 centimeters to the right and draw a parallel line. Connect those two lines in the middle.

H

3. Draw a pair of parallel 4-centimeter vertical lines. Make a diagonal line from the top of the left-hand line to the bottom of the right-hand one.

N

4. Draw a 5-centimeter vertical line. From the top of that line draw a 3-centimeter perpendicular line to the right. From the middle of that line draw a 2-centimeter perpendicular line to the right. (SUGGESTION: Explain that the meaning of the last sentence changes depending on whether "MIDDLE" or "THAT" is stressed.)

F

This exercise will give you practice solving a number problem. Listen carefully and work the problem as you go. (SUGGESTION: Explain to the students that they should work this problem from top to bottom, not left to right.)

In the upper left-hand corner of your paper write down a 30. Multiply by 5. Subtract 16. Your answer now has three numbers. <u>Copy</u> the smallest one in the upper right-hand corner of your paper. Add 80. Subtract 28. Multiply by 2. What's the answer?

$$
\begin{array}{r}
30 \\
\times 5 \\
\hline
150 \\
-16 \\
\hline
134
\end{array}
$$

$$
\begin{array}{r}
1 \\
+80 \\
\hline
81 \\
-28 \\
\hline
53 \\
\times 2 \\
\hline
106
\end{array}
$$

This exercise will give you practice solving a number problem. Listen carefully and work the problem as you go.

In the upper left-hand corner of your paper write down a 17. Add 60. Subtract 13. Multiply by 2. Your answer now has three numbers. Copy the middle one in the upper right-hand corner of your paper. Add 80. Subtract 26. Divide by 8. What's the answer?

$$\begin{array}{r} 17 \\ +60 \\ \hline 77 \\ -13 \\ \hline 64 \\ \times 2 \\ \hline 128 \end{array}$$

$$\begin{array}{r} 2 \\ +80 \\ \hline 82 \\ -26 \\ \hline 8\overline{)56} \\ 7 \end{array}$$

(SUGGESTION: When you put this answer on the board explain that the way the division is done here is not standard in the US. It's used only to make things simpler.)

This exercise will give you practice solving a number problem. Listen carefully and work the problem as you go.

In the upper right-hand corner of your paper write down a 28. Divide by 4. Add 40. Multiply by 5. Your answer now has three <u>digits.</u> Copy the right-hand one in the upper left-hand corner. Square that number. Add 50. Divide by 5. What's your answer?

$$5^2$$
$$\overline{25}$$
$$+50$$
$$5\,\lfloor\overline{75}$$
$$15$$

$$4\,\lfloor 28$$
$$\overline{7}$$
$$+40$$
$$\overline{47}$$
$$\times 5$$
$$\overline{235}$$

(SUGGESTION: When you put this answer on the board explain that the way the division is done here is not standard in the US. It's used only to make things simpler.)

This exercise will give you practice solving a number problem. Listen carefully and work the problem as you go.

In the upper left-hand corner of your paper write down a 35. Add 29. Find the square root. Multiply by 16. Your answer now has three numbers. Copy the biggest digit in the upper right-hand corner. Subtract 3. Square that answer. Add 3 and multiply by 4. What's the answer?

$$
\begin{array}{r}
35 \\
+29 \\
\hline
\sqrt{64} \\
\hline
8 \\
\times 16 \\
\hline
128
\end{array}
\qquad\qquad
\begin{array}{r}
8 \\
-3 \\
\hline
5^2 \\
\hline
25 \\
+3 \\
\hline
28 \\
\times 4 \\
\hline
112
\end{array}
$$

This exercise will give you practice solving a number problem. Listen carefully and work the problem as you go.

In the upper right-hand corner of your paper write down a 17. Add 16. Multiply by 6. Subtract 4. Your answer now has three digits. Underline the biggest one. Copy it in the upper left-hand corner. Find the square root. Multiply by 40 and subtract 16. What's your answer?

$$\sqrt{9}$$
$$\overline{3}$$
$$\times 40$$
$$\overline{120}$$
$$-16$$
$$\overline{104}$$

$$17$$
$$+16$$
$$\overline{33}$$
$$\times 6$$
$$\overline{198}$$
$$-4$$
$$\overline{194}$$

This exercise will give you practice in solving a problem. Listen carefully and follow the directions.

Draw a circle with a 5-centimeter diameter. Bisect it from top to bottom and left to right. In the upper left-hand sector put a 40. In the lower right-hand sector put a 15. In the upper right-hand sector put an A. Now add the numbers together and put your answer in the remaining sector.

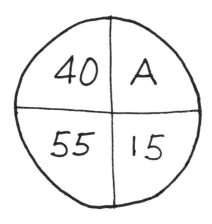

This exercise will give you practice solving a problem. Listen carefully and follow the directions.

Draw a square with a 6-centimeter base. Divide it into four equal smaller squares. In the lower left-hand square write a 13. In the square diagonally opposite that put a 28. In the lower right-hand square put a 17. Now subtract the smallest number from the biggest one and put your answer in the empty square.

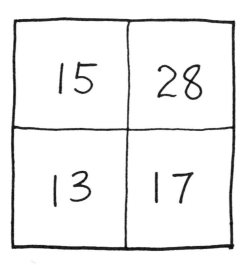

This exercise will give you practice solving a problem. Listen carefully and follow the directions.

Draw a circle with a 5-centimeter diameter. Bisect it <u>both ways.</u> In the upper right-hand sector put a 49. Put a 16 in the sector below that. In the sector to the left of that put a 36. Now find the square root of each number. Add the answers together and put your new answer in the other square.

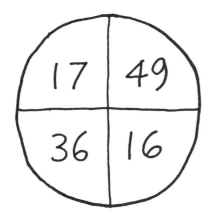

This exercise will give you practice solving a problem. Listen carefully and follow the directions.

Draw a 4-centimeter square and bisect it both ways. To the right of it draw a circle with a 4-centimeter diameter. Bisect it from left to right. In the upper right-hand square put a 19. Diagonally opposite that put a 38. Put a 28 in the square beneath the 19. Divide the biggest number by the smallest one and write your answer in the upper half of the circle.

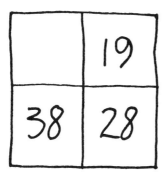 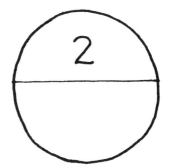

This exercise will give you practice solving a problem. Listen carefully and follow the directions.

Draw a 6-centimeter circle and bisect it both ways. In the lower left-hand sector write a 72. Put a 15 in the sector above that and a 63 in the sector to the right of it. Add the two biggest numbers together. Divide by the smallest one and put your answer in the remaining sector.

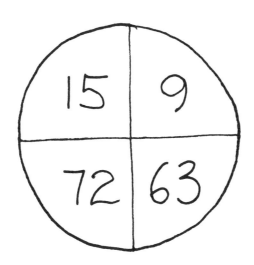

This exercise will give you practice solving a number problem. Listen carefully and work the problem as you go.

In the upper left-hand corner of your paper write down a 15. Subtract 3. Multiply by 8. Add 53. Your answer how has 3 digits. Circle the biggest one. Add the other two together and put that answer in the upper right-hand corner. Multiply by 16. Add 1 and find the square root. What's your answer?

```
  15              5
 - 3           x16
  12            80
 x 8           + 1
  96           √81
 +53            9
 14⑨
```

This exercise will give you practice solving a number problem. Listen carefully and work the problem as you go.

In the upper right-hand corner of your paper write down a 40. Subtract 6. Multiply by 4 and add 28. Your answer now has three digits. Subtract the smallest one from the biggest one and put that answer in the other top corner. Add 3. Square that number. Multiply by 2. What's the answer?

$$
\begin{array}{r}
5 \\
+\ 3 \\
\hline
8 \\
\hline
64 \\
\times\ 2 \\
\hline
128
\end{array}
\qquad
\begin{array}{r}
40 \\
-\ 6 \\
\hline
34 \\
\times\ 4 \\
\hline
136 \\
+28 \\
\hline
164
\end{array}
$$

This exercise will give you practice solving a number problem. Listen carefully and work the problem as you go.

In the upper left-hand corner of your paper put a 49. Multiply by 5. Add 134. Your answer now has three digits. Draw a circle around the biggest one. Copy the digit that's to the left of the circle in the upper right-hand corner. Square it and add 30. Subtract 8. What's your answer?

$$
\begin{array}{r}
49 \\
\times 5 \\
\hline
245 \\
+134 \\
\hline
37\,\textcircled{9}
\end{array}
\qquad
\begin{array}{r}
7^2 \\
\hline
49 \\
+30 \\
\hline
79 \\
-8 \\
\hline
71
\end{array}
$$

This exercise will give you practice solving a number problem. Listen carefully and work the problem as you go.

In the upper right-hand corner of your paper write a 73 and multiply it by 2. Add 205. Your answer now has three digits. Add them together and put your answer in the upper left-hand corner. Find the square root. Multiply by 27 and then subtract 16. What's the answer?

$$\sqrt{9}$$
$$\overline{3}$$
$$\times 27$$
$$\overline{81}$$
$$-16$$
$$\overline{65}$$

$$73$$
$$\times 2$$
$$\overline{146}$$
$$+205$$
$$\overline{351}$$

This exercise will give you practice solving a number problem. Listen carefully and work the problem as you go.

In the upper left-hand corner of your paper write a 113. Multiply by 5 and then subtract 16. Your answer now has three digits. Draw a circle around the biggest one. Multiply that number times the smallest one and put your answer in the upper right-hand corner. Find the square root. Add 15 and multiply by 6. What's the answer?

$$
\begin{array}{r}
113 \\
\times\ 5 \\
\hline
565 \\
-16 \\
\hline
54\,\textcircled{9}
\end{array}
$$

$$
\begin{array}{r}
\sqrt{36} \\
\hline
6 \\
+15 \\
\hline
21 \\
\times\ 6 \\
\hline
126
\end{array}
$$

This exercise will give you practice solving a problem. Listen carefully and follow the directions.

Draw a circle with a 5-centimeter diameter and bisect it both ways. In the upper right-hand sector put a 17. In the sector to the left of that put an X. In the lower left-hand sector put a 40. Write an S in the remaining sector. Add the numbers together, subtract 7 and put your answer in the sector with the X.

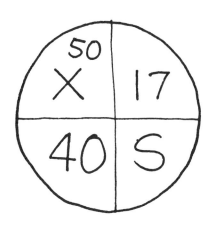

This exercise will give you practice solving a problem. Listen carefully and follow the directions.

Draw a square with a 5-centimeter base and divide it into four equal smaller squares. In the lower left-hand square write a 14. In the square above that make a G and an 8. In the square to the right of that put a Z and a 13. Add the lower left-hand number to the number in G and put your answer in the empty square.

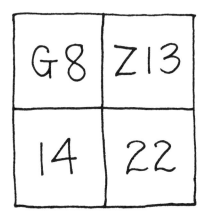

This exercise will give you practice solving a problem. Listen carefully and follow the directions.

Draw a 4-centimeter circle and bisect it from top to bottom and left to right. Beneath it draw a triangle with a 4-centimeter base and a 5-centimeter height. Bisect it from top to bottom. In the upper left-hand sector of the circle put a 25. Below that write a 17. Diagonally opposite that put an 82. Now add all the numbers together and put your answer in the right-hand part of the triangle.

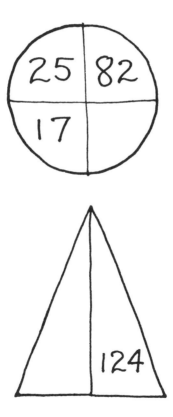

This exercise will give you practice solving a problem. Listen carefully and follow the directions.

> Draw a 4-centimeter circle followed by a 4-centimeter square. Bisect them both both ways. in the upper right-hand sector of the circle make an F. Put a 40 in the sector below that. In the lower left-hand square write a 39. In the square to the right of that write an A. in the lower left-hand sector of the circle put a 21. now add all the numbers together and put your answer in the upper left-hand part of the square.

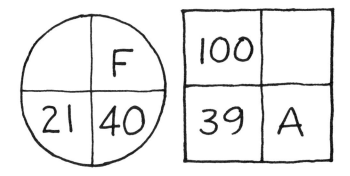

This exercise will give you practice putting shapes in the right place. It's long and kind of hard. Listen carefully and follow the directions.

Draw a circle with a 10-centimeter diameter. In the middle of the circle draw a triangle with a 1-centimeter base and a 2-centimeter height. Below the triangle draw a rectangle with a 2-centimeter height and a 4-centimeter base. Bisect the rectangle from left to right. Now draw a 2-centimeter circle one centimeter above and two centimeters to the right of the apex of the triangle. Make another circle of the same size in the same place on the other side of the triangle. Make a 1-centimeter circle inside each of the bigger ones. One centimeter above the big left-hand circle draw a 2-centimeter diagonal line from the bottom left to the top right. Draw a diagonal line going the opposite way above the big right-hand circle.